THAT
DADA
STRAIN

Also by Jerome Rothenberg

Poems

Translations

Anthologies

Recordings

Prose

THAT DADA STRAIN

JEROME ROTHENBERG

A NEW DIRECTIONS BOOK

ACKNOWLEDGMENTS

Grateful acknowledgment is made to the editors and publishers of magazines and books in which some of the material in this volume previously appeared: *Artful Dodge, Boundary 2, Conjunctions, Crawl Out Your Window, Doc(k)s, Flexible Flyer, In'hui* (Amiens), *New Wilderness Letter, O.ARS, Pen Pals, The Red Hand Book* (ed. Tom Patterson Pynyon Press, Atlanta), *Roadwork, Shirim, Spar, Spectacular Diseases* (London), *Sulfur, Text,* and *Trumps.*

Portions of this book appeared as separate publications (books and broadsides) by Jerome Rothenberg and are reprinted here by permission of the publishers: Ken Mikolowski and Alternative Press (*A Poem—Maybe a Dream—for Travelers*), Kimball Higgs, Harvy Polkinhorn, and Atticus Press (*Imaginal Geography 9* and *That Dada Strain*), Debra Weier and Emanon Press (*A Merz Sonata, for Kurt Schwitters*), the Folger Shakespear Library (*That Dada Strain*), Matthew Tyson and Spot Press (*Two Sonnets 1980* and *The History of Dada As My Muse*), and George Quasha, Patricia Nedds, and Station Hill Press (*A New Testament* and "Hunger" and "The Little Saint of Huautla" from *Altar Pieces* by Jerome Rothenberg).

"Zurich Chronicle 1915–1919" by Tristan Tzara and "Merz" (1920) by Kurt Schwitters are quoted courtesy of George Wittenborn, Inc.; "L'Art" (1920) is quoted courtesy of Madame Olga Picabia.

Manufactured in the United States of America
First published as New Directions Paperbook 550 in 1983
Published simultaneously in Canada by George J. McLeod, Ltd., Toronto

Library of Congress Cataloging in Publication Data
Rothenberg, Jerome, 1931–
    The Dada strain.
    (A New Directions Book)
    I. Title.
PS3568.O86D3   1983   811'.54   82-18827
ISBN 0-8112-0860-5 (pbk.)

New Directions Books are published for James Laughlin
by New Directions Publishing Corporation
80 Eighth Avenue, New York 10011

CONTENTS

In a poetry reading, the voice carries the poet's equivalent of an oral tradition, speaking things the written poem has left unsaid. Does this betray the poem? we used to wonder. Or does it allow an audience of strangers to share some of what is so obvious to the poet that it enters into the poem as something wholly natural—what cannot & should not be omitted? In my own world—let us say—the DADA fathers who inhabit the opening poems of this book are necessary figures, & to summon them up along with their legends is no more erudite an act than to summon up Moses or George Washington or Harpo or Karl Marx, & so on. But I can't assume, when I turn to Tzara or to Hugo Ball, say, a common tradition that would be shared with any group of listeners I might be addressing—so I begin my reading by saying: This is a poem for Hugo Ball, who founded the Cabaret Voltaire in Zurich 1916 & went off into the hills of Switzerland to die there as a kind of Catholic DADA saint. It is all a question of a handle & a desire (in spite of the poem's final mystery) to be truly understood.

The work is clear to me in its named persons & places—if less so in its imaginal figures or its syntax. In the present instance the first force I would summon up is that of a DADA movement nearly seventy years into its history. Its authors have passed, as Blake would have said, into "eternity," to become the fathers of imaginal acts done in their memory. The spirit that remains is the final resistance to the tyranny of one's own works, as it emerges in Tzara's manifesto insistence that "the true Dadas are against Dada." The measure of their failure (& of ours) is in the degree of divergence from their most defiant aim: "the liberation of the creative forces from the tutelage of the advocates of power."

At the end of *Vienna Blood*, I found myself coming back to Tzara & to DADA—a step that Diane Wakoski described as my having taken DADA for my *muse*, not (she said) "a lady with wings floating around the house [but] whatever really interests you, turns you on and keeps you from turning in on

vii

yourself." As such, the DADAs appeared to me both as children & (in a reading of their name that they denied themselves) as fathers—literally the generation of my own father. Dead & gone now, they arise like him in retrospect as total lives: Ball as the shaman-priest turned saint described above; Schwitters renaming DADA "Merz" & erecting in his Hanover house an expanded sculptural memorial to DADA before his wartime flight to Norway & England (Ambleside); & Picabia as playboy DADA moving through worlds on both sides of the Atlantic as pope of a new & nonexistent DADA Church. The Covering Cherub—coming to me from Blake & Ezekiel in my own polemic against anti-DADA critic Harold Bloom—is the sure image of authority & repression (church & state) that keep us from the construction of new languages & worlds.

No one, of course, is really DADA now, but the resistance (as long as it continues) may take enough of a backward look to consider those who came before us. Viewed in this way, their leading edge would seem to be through language—its collapse & reconstruction—that led them to invent new languages (like Ball's wordless poetry) in which would be fulfilled Apollinaire's prophecy: "victory will be above all / to see truly into the distance / to see everything / up close / so that everything can have a new name." In my own case, I find myself working at this from two obvious sources—what seems to have little reference outside my own language & perceptions, & what follows closely from the visions & the language acts of others. Unlike most of the poems in the opening section, those in "Imaginal Geographies" take the first path & want no further explanation. In that way they are reflections of procedures shared with the Dada poets & others—for linking words by letter, number, shape, & sound, or for recording associations between images for which no key is readily available, if it ever was.

The last section of the book is my attempt to fight against even this fascination with language—to return to the world in which human beings still suffer both for the loss of bread & words. At readings I find, however much the elements within them move & collide, that I can deliver most of these poems straight. The exceptions, possibly, involve references to Yaqui

Easter ceremonies at which I spent four days among Chapayeka clowns & blackveiled Roman soldiers, seeing behind the comic figures a world of fantasized Jews (but never named as such), who raised memories for me of images from my own *Poland/ 1931*—or, in the final poem, a visit to the Mazatec shamaness Maria Sabina, whose chanted poetry & sense of yet another "collapse of language" I had elsewhere helped to bring to light. Behind both of these events, I felt the presence in traditional form of what poets in our own culture have long pursued: an entry to what the Yaquis so beautifully call "enchanted world" or "flower world," or Maria Sabina, from a still different perspective, "the book of language."

Finally, I would point out that the title of the book, *That Dada Strain,* doesn't come from European DADA at all but from jazz & blues traditions of the 1920s—specifically as the title of a still surviving early jazz standard. I would take that coincidence as clearly "dada," even kabbalistic, & would let it go at that.

Jerome Rothenberg
October 1982

1 / That Dada Strain

THAT DADA STRAIN

the zig zag mothers of the gods
of science   the lunatic fixed stars
& pharmacies
fathers who left the tents of anarchism
unguarded
the arctic bones
strung out on saint germain
like tom toms
living light bulbs
aphrodisia
"art is junk" the urinal
says "dig a hole
"& swim in it"
a message from the grim computer
"ye are hamburgers"

February 1916 In the most obscure of streets in the shadow of archi-
tectural ribs, where you will find discreet detectives amid red street
lamps—birth—birth of the Cabaret Voltaire—personages in one edi-
tion appear, recite or commit suicide, bustle and stir, the joy of the
people, cries, the cosmopolitan mixture of god and brothel, the crys-
tal and the fattest woman in the world: "Under the Bridges of Paris."
(T. Tzara)

THE HISTORY OF DADA AS MY MUSE

the history of the fathers
is only Dada time   only yesterday
only the day before
the morning after, time
spent in this century
an empty train
snaking its way to Paris
cathedral where an old sump overflows
that leaves them dizzy
shit sticking to their cuffs
unpressed but with the fathers' zest
for living   vests & monocles
proclaim an avant garde
in absence an avant garde proclaims
itself   the young men
fathers of the history of Dada
still ride its rails
rise past my eiffel towers
at each bump
each anal urge propels them
"this is the heart of culture"
they proclaim
the heart of war
the Dada god's heart
in the world their poems make
muses drum on walls
on saddles
muses masturbate into the wind
o Dada o my Muse
the young men under cellophane
sleep with the history of the fathers
in the fathers' heads
a girl named Schopenhauer dances
the train to Paris lands in Zanzibar
verses come upside down

to free us   verses
reversals in the history of language
voice
divine
foot
solitude
the king of islands in a tree
a fiddle in each hand
his sex implanted in midst of branches
upsets their tables, spills
his dreams along the floor
the sounds of queens in books
young men—the fathers—walk by
each is the other's muse
waits with a shadowed lady
at his side
footballs thrown between
the fathers
float past the empty trainyards
only yesterday
in somebody else's dream
the voice unlocked, reversed
the figure halfway inside the window
cut in two
the train in the revolver's mouth
baffled by other trains
by cogwheels
an assemblage of spare parts
can never suit
                  the fathers
the fathers can never suit themselves
by banging   each man
is the other's muse
each is his own football
over Paris   waving
from a perch above the opera
holds a mackerel in each hand
blue lights above them

the jellied colors of their gods
o Nostrodamus
is your first name Jerome
like mine?
is Sagittarius our brother?
where are the proud Apaches
now?   the sons
of Dada?
on a billboard
Paris waits
the history of the century
illuminated, grey
in moonlight
welcomes my Muse as Dada
military bands spatter the station
they screw my muse
paper septembers o voltaic arc
true & blue
electric
shock
grey life
the Dadaist rides up an elevator
with the pope
the fathers adrift like muses
down one eiffel tower
up the next
o light wheels teeming with blue ants
what began as Dada ends
as Dadahood
as my hand ends, halfway
waving
halfway cut off from its fingers
where the street ends
where another street turns halfway
into another street

23.vi.16

For that evening's reading he had made himself a special costume. His legs were in a shiny blue cylinder, which came up to his hips so that he looked like an obelisk. Over it he wore a huge coat collar cut out of cardboard, scarlet inside and gold outside. It was fastened at the neck in such a way that he could give the impression of winglike movement by raising and lowering his elbows. He also wore a high, blue-and-white-striped witch doctor's hat.

A GLASS TUBE ECSTASY

for Hugo Ball

a glass tube
for my leg   says Hugo Ball
my hat a cylinder
in blue & white
the night   the german ostriches   the sink
he pisses in
all these become his world
his dada song, begun there
holds the image
until it comes at us:
the image from its cross
looks down:
a ribbon
a revolver
mud
these contribute
to his death
also to what his death contributes
later, too hysterical
too sick with god
& time:
a carousel
a roasted poet

7

fish
the queen says to his mind
& enters
where the street of mirrors starts
she sees his face
reflected
in hunger of the world
as pain, the consciousness
of death   not why we die
but why we dream about it
& why our dreams can't save
the dying remnant
Hugo
as I write this poem
the voice cries
from a further room
the dancer / singer calls me
from a further room
I step into an obelisk
below the waist
my mouth opens to sing
but freezes
shut
in grief for you
ombula
takē
bitdli
solunkola
the collapse of language
tabla tokta tokta takabala
taka tak
a glass tube ecstasy
escapes from time
babula m'balam
the image & the word
over your bed
hang   crucified
again the cabaret explodes

again again
fatigue
one
foot
in glass
a glass nerve
&
a priestly gas pump
pulls
her hair out

A MERZ SONATA

for Kurt Schwitters

world of the crying man
is death's world
money acids him, he sucks
hard on his tongue
but can't unjunct the word
therefore he stows his house
shovels the floor
a column shivers skywards
the man can stride down
crying: **MERZ!**
sweet Kurt's word
column overstacked with
mirrors   pretzels
the revival of the alphabet
hustles him toward England
cuckoos Dada journeys
in painted car
van Doesburg springs a **merz** hand
a **merz** gesture
drips   **merz** bodies
wet & tumored
prong the **merz** girls
tip into their shallow holes
& provocate
streamers of wet **merz**
merz merchants
line the streets with—
commercial **merzers**
merzing in a ring
their products
sauce & ciders
jars
delirious as number two's
he slabs onto his roof

o coupons
tiny tickets
we trade off with burgermeisters
bits of shoelace
half-stapled cigarettes
a worm   a fish
merz angels swing from
tangled in air
nail parings
slice of tie
mimosa orange tulpe flora aphrodite
bottles alight with piss
& baking soda
merzd in his slots
a pot of water
—boiling—
you can drop a clock in
watch it converge to ice
or noodles
squawking german from full throat
der fisch dill schreizen karpenblut
heil hitler
makes a **merz**-poem
fidill schreifi karblu
makes a poem
a **merz**-poem makes a fiddle
marchers **merz**
merz marches
behind the band—boom boom—o
little Dada towns
devoured by incest
still more devoured by holes
by calendars
merz christmas trees spruced up
merz stickers pasted on **merz** walls
merz slogans:
du du
and

and du du
a n n a b l u m e
and
and **merz**
My Valentine!
keep burning on & on
Get GLOWING
Thou
thine eye prays
yearns my eye
thou art my yearn
I acid thou
I far thou
sideways slides his stem into
her slit
her slot makes bubbles
rise over his column
where the babe's head hides them
barking to the crowds
the tall man is the crying man
—bow wow—
the generals are swooning
as he sings
sweet **merz** songs
making their cradles rock
their prussian wives wipe dribbles
from their cheeks
& dream bavarian cushions
they can lunge their stumps against
for breath   for fantasies
not like the dreams of **merz**
or freedom
but the collective eye
o you o me
o elephants o commas
o I sing for Kurt this **merz** song
o I swoon—I moon—for him

cat
    legs
catlegs & human joys
& humans world the earth roundout the cats
like jews who fiddle papers
who gurgle "anna blume" from full throats
cutouts of Hitler
paper bikers
stream down the german roads
make Norway
scramble him—crying & tall—toward Ambleside
the real disuda of the nightmare
Alabaster
death
he tries to feel by language
Why?
We
Thy
Thee
Thou
the dog barks Alabaster
drip drip
plugs the sky
pins
a little moustache to his lip
the generals are dead
the candled towers of his **merz**
explode
the dream of **merz**
—stuck in his head—
undrips him
flattens his last pretzel
to its walls
its walls
five four three two one
wall
wall

WALL
WALL WALL WALL
WALL WALL WALL
WALL   WALL   WALL   WALL
walls
walls
walls
WALLS WALLS WALLS WALLS
WALL
WALL WALL WALL
WALL WALL WALL
wall wall wall
wall
wall
wall

wall

"The word Merz had no meaning when I formed it. Now it has the meaning which I gave it. The meaning of the concept Merz changes with the change in the insight of those who continue to work with it." (K. *Schwitters*)

THE MECHANICAL BRIDE

no longer is mechanical, today
not nor tomorrow
they prop her under the tunnel
that bears her name
sad bride
thy tiny flanges swell & fall
the man who buys thy roadster
hauls thee to the dance
mechanical & beaming
like a brain machine
the pope of DADA mounts thee
sucks thy pipes
later will pop his rivets on
thy rubber cushions

February 12, 1920

"The principle of the word BEAUTY is merely an automatic and visual convention. Life has nothing to do with what the grammarians call *Beauty*. Virtue, like patriotism, exists only for the mediocre intellects who have devoted their entire lives to the tomb. This fountainhead of men and women who regard *Art* as a dogma whose *God* is the accepted convention must be dried up. We do not believe in *God*, no more than we believe in *Art*, or in its priests, bishops, and cardinals." (F. Picabia)

A PICKLE & A CROWN, PICABIA, THE POPE OF DADA

in the night the pope of DADA
wanders   in the light
the pope of DADA hides behind
his wall, his wallet
sliding down his trousers
until it drops from him
discloses
the perpetual photographs
mon cher Picabia
the girl next door, the virgin
with a weenie in each hand
metallic smell of drippy nitrates
in your mouth
first of the roadside romeos
along the imperial boulevards of Europe
playboy who twangs his mandoline
nightly, or twice a night
the pontiff's kitten
has no edge on you   Picabia
you dip
you somersault
you hop into your roadster

ballet madonna
bearded queen between the acts
who packs
a pickle & a crown
Picabia   the pope of DADA
his penis   heart-shaped   valentine
rests on our pillows
onanism is pure semiotics
o Joan of Arc my murky inkbottle
your pipes under the ladies' convent
the conduit of dreams
new plastic
buttons   like a safety valve
releasing steam
dribbles a cross atop
her buttocks
twitching   seamless
the pope shifts from one foot
to the other
smearing her holy knobs with creams
crowns her
MAMA to his DADA
offers his first hydrocruise to her
over Bermuda
where her triangle ignites
on his o snappy
virgin   mother
wearing his yachting cap
his sailor's pipe
hangs from her sphinctered mouth
"Picabia my popeyed pope of DADA"
giggles the girl child
motherless
o thermostat o clean machine
"I spread my MAMA legs for you
"I yank my fenugreek
"when you yank yours
"so squirmish like a Zulu

"I PAPA you Picabia I POPE you
"the metal bedbugs fly back to our room
"they fracture the scenery
"unbutton the priests
"fat cassocks pop like sexual desserts
"your crack & mine
"they lick   Picabia
"our stacks they blow
"they wiggle a revolver
"at my mound
"the round side of my buttocks
"flushes   immediate
"& red become
"my flaccid nodules
"the fateful pressure of his gush
"under my veils
"releases the raw gelatin   its drips
"cover my plump face
"mine are the jaws of MAMA DADA
"clipped over yours in love
"they suck up all your spigots
"& your DADA eye Picabia like mine
"scans the new lincoln coupe
"the cabriolet
"changes your ragtime into
"punk BOOMBOOM
King MAMA sings   the Cuban
music follows her
a straight line traced by a mechanical hand
it cracks the immigrant Atlantic
like a snail, unpacks
artist & bride in distant 1913
twin pigeons over Norfolk Street
—o armories—
—o woolworth towers—
city grown rife with espionage
the general's chauffeur is you
Picabia   the fiddle of the Jews

is ever fishy   making hats
my grandfather
plots his return to Poland
the crisis of the object starts
in Bayonne
millenary
madness
thinking: hats
are never hats
his brain spins like a pinwheel
a saint of saints
he calls himself   the virgin
is a sparkplug
spermal chimneys
circle the pope of DADA
words & vapors
flowers
the war is half over & the world
waits to be born again
Picabia to greet you
panting beneath your covers
in the twilight of this century
the bride's bidet
propped crownless in one corner
the sound of waves
remembered
like the tinkle of thy peepee
o my DADA love

DADAGRAM ONE

LARGE TEARS & cataracts perform   snappy & electri-
cal   in pigtails   the zigzags crackle once in gauze & once
in heavy sentences   here is the admiral   & here are twelve
children painting holy virgins on raw flesh   & here are your
diphthongs (listen!) pushing through your gut a shiny metal
gallows blossoming like a movie without lights or wires   a
house to rent the admiral the admiral is dead in   the great
magician who plants tomatoes in your forehead   who har-
vests pyramids in laundromats   feeble cylinders outside his
toll booth   the world seen through the butcher's eye is
shut   the world to come is gumbo the Dadaist beside the
pump says   his words emerging from his bearded heart   o
xylophones   o texas   x-y-z

DADAGRAM TWO

molecular like a drain & like a fire the goddess clambers up the
german chimney   mirages cucumbers emissions churning
television custards   inside the palace of the avant garde the
fattest woman in the world bends over throbs & jerks like
cheese or marmalade she showers sparks across the dance floor
peppers & palmettoes wafted up the captain's nose   *ahoy*
squeaks the Dadaist   *she is the statue of liberty & we visit
her in the imperial harbor   I am not an eagle* squeaks the
Dadaist   *& I am certainly not a bus driver* he squeaks   *not
even lately   I blossom by day in nickel & by night in plati-
num   returning twice I watch the sphinx rise from my table
caesar's shoulderblade in fragments the goddess in a wooden
apron come alive beneath red lights & maps of panama spread
on the table twin couples dance in spasms & in vestibules in
memory & in the key of g*   they know the Dadaist who
squeaks isn't the Dadaist who sleeps inside her   his head
against her iron rails   his fingers playing dada on her tinny
circuits

THE COVERING CHERUB &
THE ACADEMY OF DADA

> "I will destroy thee, O covering cherub, from the midst
> of the stones of fire."

—Ezekiel 28:16

for B., among the *minim*

1

under the angel's wing
the cherub's head
still cries
it is the babe of Schwitters' column
the last to stay
it stays here
stripped of its hair
my melancholy angel   cherub
with peacock's mouth
disturbed by dream who bellows
like cow or cormorant
bladder of the female beast
elusive   feathers
stuck to its gauzy skin
to keep us from our body's
image   it becomes
the head seen by the Senecas
in flight
the sacred yo-yo
we steel ourselves against
but feel
sting of its prickly cheeks
over our nipples
weakened
shoved to the darkest wall
the cherub has no eyes
he says   the cherub
is no sparky lady I have known

forever waited for her
called her my muse
the battle to the death is with
the cherub death
the angel death resembles
it is the babe lost in the wood
the babe's head
mangled angry fetus
screaming for death among the outlaws
priests of the academy
of DADA   exile
is the true pain
that the cherub leads to   death
is in his language
but beside the cherub stands
the other the false cherub
that the cherub will become
now   that the cherub is
too weak to speak it
his words a shadow of his words
a cat-light glowing
like babe made out of words
the cherub vomits
sadly
into the cherub's death

2 THE ACADEMY OF DADA

knows not Alexandria nay nay nor Athens
knows not even deluxe prime puritan hotshot miltonic
mudcats, these the ACADEMY OF DADA
knows not   nor knows the academy nay nay
why some cherubic jewboys seek out the gentile lights
to illumine therewith the jewish darkness blind synagogue
lonely among their throngs nay nay the ACADEMY OF DADA
knows not such pith yet knows it Tzara's ghost in oldtime
     Dada journeys
landeth in Zurich schoolboy-fresh another midget oriental

Dada disgust foretold erupts his spontaneity against
the bandits killers who suck from our still throats
what honeys! precious pollens he restores to earth
ferocious unrequited Sammy Rosenstock who standeth hatless
among the goyim terrors of the nation-
state the cherub is who is true cherub
but the ACADEMY OF DADA
knows not the least green vales of England nor knows cathedral
     bells
ding dong it is the first academy without a book
only the sky a solitary Dada cloud pinned to its cardboard
crying: death to alabaster!
long live the ACADEMY OF DADA!
tra la its priests poach from each other's pockets, singly
singingly they bang on their computers
light up like soft machines bounce b.b.'s over metal counters
acrobats slide down academic tubes the ACADEMY OF DADA
knows not umbrellas neither knows it love in bloom
nay nay nor bloom in love yet croons still over Anna Blumë
day by day over Rrose Selavy by night & knows not
where the cherub walks planting amid his trees the fear of
     Dada
Dada knows not but knows each is his own Dada
each wears a Dada hat that shines
like Dada symphonies
& Dada ice-creams
each brings his Dada song alive where Dada
knows not Dada lives on in spirit of the world
o freedom of the mind the line o freedom of the heart
from hunger solitude
(he cries)
"to free the forces of poesis from
"the gods of power
"let the cherub's wing fall   pull
"the cherub through the mud of paradise
"out of the sacred grove

THE SUICIDE OF DADA

the man I would address as father is at last
my son's age, as the light advances
through the century & comes to rest
—static & pale light—
this moment when the clarity of Dada
opens anew to us   o zygote
energies   impeccable & greased wheels
we have assembled in America
will make a kind of music from it
fast-stepping & scarcely true
but beautiful
the young man struts before his mirror
even now   he brushes
his kinky hair into a black wave
adjusts his monocle a third time
spits into his palm
as though his hand said: watch my fingers
curl round this stick
& widen
then watch my bukovina eyes
—forever blue—
—forever dopey—
waiting to gawk at you
tomorrow in light of cabaret
my zigzag balladeers
will blow into your boots
like midget bikers they will celebrate
the suicide of Dada
as it falls out every twenty years (or thirty)
will squawk into his public ear
his pubis still alive
& bouncy
o my ecstatic Dada father cleave for me
the obsessive grey intestines of your nightmare
wrapped round our throats
like logic like a throbbing liquid plant

space-devils controlled by agents from the moon
the generals of America & Russia
who stomp on us
will hear about it in their map rooms
first   their galleries a decade later
they who once watched the Dada kid
strut before hundreds
saw him hitch tie up to adam's apple
his heavy collar fallen to his chest
o talking tie   *for Ed Sanders*
o toe drum
dumb Dada with your droopy eyes
not yet the rich man's Dada
Dada looking into Dada's face
in love with Dadahood as power
Dada powerless
the ritual of work reborn as Dada
Dada reborn as death
his dancing feet have trod on marshmallows
thousands of times
on burning ladders he has sat
has pissed on Dada
still marching to that Dada strain
the procession of the fathers enters for the last time
the caverns of the cabaret
become a disco now   Ed
where the Dada fathers edge their way
banging the walls
the spirits of rich painters cry from
o generations now alive & dead
in the most obscure of streets
(he writes)
lit by red street lamps
they yammer to the dancers in new languages
bang! bang!
Dada disgust ignites the keyboard
playing tiger rock
through telephones
a few poems read out loud

Da Dada da da dadadadadada
etc.
last week I saw
in boundaries of New Pascua
still alive
old clown
old Yaqui fat face
the man I would address as father
mean & fat
offers his fingers to the audience
captains & mechanics
the designers of a failed poetics
they lift a chair into the air
on which the bride sits
she whom we call the mind
already free
takes flight across the ages
of his suicide   escapes
the bankers & muses of the rich
past the terrors of their mindlessness
still cannot hear the drum tattoo
the way his hips shake
moving the black hooves
cocoons of butterflies
the despair of vacuum cleaners from behind the altar
turns to laughter
now returns us to our flower worlds
the shady lady & the Dada financiers
committing suicide
mark the beginnings of
the death of
DADA
the judas clown who bangs the auto hood
opens the Dada wilderness
vanilla sparks & lights he wafts to us
like flowers   tattooed goat turds
their Dada deaths & victories
passed down the generations
to reach our common shore

2/ Imaginal Geographies

A NEW TESTAMENT

"you are no different
"than the rest   the Jew says
to the Jew, his brother
in the exquisite field of Jewishness
the haven of lost rabbi-
shamans, brave searchers for
the Law of Language
the fiction of the primal book
averted, like his eyes
darting behind the wall
who falls & whispers:
"feathers"   "frankincense"
in the true language of their god

TWO SONNETS: 1980

1

it is better to receive
the friend says
oddly   surely   certainly
they drum the poem back
into the earth
of california   the poem
remembered by its silences
the words drop out
empty & useless
the car barrels down the freeway
eating the last
french fried potato   *for Emmett Williams*
old scraps of satisfaction
from a friend

2

I love the fingers
of the rain, they melt
over my eyes
the train gets here at noon
a crowd of sun bathers
tickles the ocean
scissors cut a landscape
eggs & stars
hello   goodbye
we sing, we twist
the mussels from these rocks
holding the coast
mad california grows for us
another year

THREE IMAGINAL GEOGRAPHIES

1

the drowned men in your hills
messiahs   cupids
lie on their curtained beds

& move
no muscle not a single eye
can stare back

the ones who fall through space
fall with clocks
beside them, aren't falling

but at rest asleep
their fathers tell them: take the dream
wherever it ends

the dream will hold you
weightless
you'll learn to fly

again your arms
riding along the surface
of a wave

a star will follow you
back to a time so solid
it becomes a thing

a thing becomes an image
in your head
your heart

becomes a clock at rest
beside you
the little moments ticking

as your throat ticks
& whispers its own language
half awake

2

the old man has
no name
he rises with the wind

maybe he follows you
"watch out"
the wall calls back to him

without a name
—the wall—
—the old man—

twisted space is senseless
but the mind
can pass it, can pass it

& past the mind
the images
still hidden wait

they pretend a fire
at the limits of
the world

no distances are real
no old men
& no walls

no stars are real

3

the universe will vanish
—nightly it does—

someday your dreams will be
the world

the star farthest from you
will be your clock

THE ABSENCE OF MIRRORS

1

there's no honest barber
in this town
no house ready for daybreak
or religion

no band ready for its madness
kling klang
music
the drummers bend & strive

riding on drums
a double
heart
how strange, voluptuous

never so steady
for departure
says the salad captain:
come with me

2

the lady
opens her mouth   a moon
balanced on tongue
a tongue pushing through blossoms

into the words *she* sounds
the light breaks:
I am this one
I am not the moon

the messenger
isn't the shipwreck:
fallen
day moves in around them

we are *them*
who play games, situate
the pronouns
under our tongues

SEVEN PORTRAITS

The Actor

bangs his son over
the knuckles   laughing

they call him Mister Toosh
the grandfather

magician of diasporas
the singing Jew

The Man with a Camera

smiles & whistles
makes them watch a fig
between his fingers
nestled

snow rests on his overcoat
his fingers in their gloves
dream of last summer
at onset of the gentile year

ding dong the catholic
bells sing to his ears:
the tears of Mary
preserved eternally on film

The Accountant

loves the rabbi's
daughter
though they cannot
dance or touch

he waits behind the door
another year
& finds her later
going crazy

The Salesman

moves his hand
over the chessboard

it is empty
the pieces are in his coat

his coat is on the chair
next to the stove

the stove is underneath
the singing kettle

The Doctor

speaks to their tongues:
how pink some are
how white some others are

who has a blue tongue?
asks the doctor
no one will tell

but the mothers walk along
the road to Warsaw:
tired feet & shoes

a sabbath morning
& a cross of ice
over the doctor's door

The Socialist

obscure & brown
the book kept between
pale fingers
drops down

signals a trail
out to the square
she follows after, sees
the workers marching

in her throat
their voices ring
her voice, open to speech
will speak for them

The Baker

at the entrance
to the bakery

a half moon hovers
like the baker's face
far from his window

smooth & yellow
is the baker's moon

a single letter
set above his cheek
under his eye

an aleph burning
black on white

DREAM POEM. I am walking past a wall on which a poster with my face on it is many times repeated. I am on my way to the airport.

11.xii.79

MORE IMAGINAL GEOGRAPHIES

1

because the rock stands there
the man sits on it
& sings:
because his eye sees the rock
& sees it again
he waits by the road
dreaming   singing
repository of the world's poor
himself in his own dream
singing in his dream

2

the eye, too late
the other eye, too late
& practical:
does a vision come to him?
a vision walks
along the road, another vision
waits back of the door:
the pain of being
doubly human
is another vision:
sometimes it sleeps with him
& calls
into his troubled ear:
o friend o human brother
there are no lights

A POEM—MAYBE A DREAM—FOR TRAVELERS

pale eyes   the tree
is friendly
even a little slow
friend Jerome he says
my watch says
3:15
I walk to the old corner of Main Street
past the Seneca
Theater & cross
the bridge *hello*
you citizens
of Salamanca
hello the dog says
he is the tree's friend
& mine
he is a silly yellow
color   eyes are shining
lightly into eyes
in Yucatan the skies are never
empty & the trees
of Yucatan talk Mayan
someone tells us:
you are going on a trip

DREAM POEM

A dream that I'm giving a lecture—to Antin & Einzig & others
—in which I tie up *angst* with Keats's "negative capability."
"Don't you know what *angst* is? It's being in doubt all the
time. It's the uncertainty principle. If you think about the
world, you live in terror. Overlooking the abyss you wait to
die. To open your mind, your throat, into a scream that lasts
forever. Whatever forever there is. And even then you're prob-
ably deluding yourself." As I say all that (& more) I feel myself
growing angry but always in control: very eloquent & very pas-
sionate.

A night full of dreams. Can't drop off to sleep without dream-
ing.
Sleepy. Letting the dreams disappear.

Tomorrow: 47 years old.

DREAM POEM

We are leaving the hotel & I can't find the mailbox with my
name on it. David Antin comes up & pulls a paper or his keys
from a box around the middle of the alphabet. He says: "I'm
listed under *H*emiroff"—he pauses—"but spellt with a J, like
in Spanish." Then what am I listed under? I continue to
search. It has the feeling of a spy novel.

DREAM POEM 20.xii.78

I was at a Catholic bar mitzvah—a ceremony I had heard of in a previous dream. They held it in a large room with several rows of tables at which boys & girls were being given sacramental wine. Visitors were welcome, but the Jewish ones at least were very nervous—"more nervous about this than about the other Catholic ceremonies," someone said. "It touches home because they all remember their own bar mitzvahs." I saw my cousin Sam outside the door but he signaled that he wouldn't go in. I was standing at the side with Matthew & was telling him that this was once a Jewish ritual. I had expected the Catholic version to be austere & regimented, but the celebrants were very noisy, almost out of control. No one was taking it seriously, not even the nuns who served them wine. Some looked bored or hostile—but wasn't the Mass even more boring, I thought or said. Many of the participants & some of the observers—mostly teen-age kids themselves—wore crosses. Was I the only one who looked Jewish? The people around me were telling anti-Catholic jokes. I strained to hear a funny story about Jesus, but I couldn't make it out. The one who told it—a boy I remembered from college days in Michigan—said he would tell me later.

DREAM POEM 7.x.78

I had escaped from prison with a young man whose name was "Mess" or "Messerschmidt." There were other details to the escape but now they've faded, & all I can remember is a door I couldn't close & that we stood there in the corridor & wondered if they would know from the door—open & swinging—that we had escaped from them. Worries as we walked along the street, which at first was a street I used to live on in the

Bronx—Gunhill Road, I think—& then another from around there, something like Rochambeau Avenue. I who was older had the most to lose. If I was captured, the years added to my sentence would amount to nearly the rest of my life. I wanted to explain to "Mess," but he was in conversation with another young man, & I became distracted. As I trailed behind, I saw the image of my face—as old as Hemingway, I thought—reflected in the shining windows of an airport. Then the streets grew European, & I thought I saw the two young men go into a house whose low windows opened on the corner of the street. A busy intersection. I looked inside & saw a young man standing near a bed, undressing. Brushing past me, two other young men were entering the building through an open door. I thought I caught an angry look from them & backed away. Onto a crowded boulevard, where the crowds kept pushing me. I wanted to find the others or to return to prison. I shouted in a very loud voice: MESSERSCHMIDT! And a young man & woman stopped beside me & told me angrily to stop making so much noise. I told them that I was looking for my friend, & they walked away. I was acutely aware of being in a foreign city.

DREAM POEM

riding the trolley line
through streets of
Salamanca
past the new subway stop
where crowds of Indians
emerge   dark grains of maize
still in my fist
the dead of Salamanca
rise   my mouth
fills up
with songs & tears

NOTE. This was a recurrent dream both I & my wife have had since leaving Salamanca—small city on the Allegany Seneca Reservation & with none of the big-town features that turn up here in dream form. But on May 7, 1982, after a couple of years away, I found myself wide-awake & driving from the Steamburg settlement toward Salamanca, expecting as usual for the expressway (still incomplete, I thought) to break off & lead me by local streets into the Indian end of town. It was then—like one of those dreams—that I saw unfamiliarly large & flashy street lamps up ahead & realized—as I drove past them & then the previously nonexistent McDonald's to my far left across from the Indian Museum—that I was strangely & unfamiliarly bypassing the city. Unlike the dream, I was able to swing back on the new stretch of expressway & reach familiar ground.

MORE IMAGINAL GEOGRAPHIES

10.vii.80

1

into the yard
exterior & interior
movements
hardly distinguished
but feared
the sun, overhead
in time & temper
winds its way around
the candy sky
no heros lean on
forgetting
the intervening passage
& return

2

they give themselves some light
a sure place
& a poor place
they are spooked by
as in their word for "home"
pure gold in any tongue
even theirs, however meager
like their lives
a place called home
marked by shadows
& a fence

GASP! GASP!

1

the dog—because he
can't talk—rubs
against the rug:
I've got a voice for you
—I think—
your belly in my mind

2

I've got a mind for you
—I think—
your belly in my voice

CABALA CAPERS

1

the old man learns to dance
"cabala capers"
it is the way his leg lifts
slowly   then a sharp kick
turns it back on him
exquisite man
& sentimental lady
in your eyes I see
illumined
the angel in the urethra
descend & glow
I lock the key inside me
I will never drop it
blindly
in the magician's hand

2

a paper star
on paper
gold or golden green
green star of sleep
green sleep lit by a star
green heart
a paper sun
crumpled
a parachute
green motors
it is spring again
again they see us walking
with the deacons
green buttons on your skin
green temperatures

the breast of heaven on the earth
your breast is green
my hand against your hand
is green

3

the bird inside
the bird's nest
burdened by cries of "kingdom"
turns its wheel
back on itself the wheel turns
brighter than the bird
the bird's nest
bursts into a hundred lights
these lights (the light says)
are letters for your name
your name dear mother father
is the name for light

MICE & DUENDE

no force this duende
but a thing this duende

substance oozing from a handwound
mice in corners
lashing other mice

no eyes this duende
but the veins in eyes this duende

duende children hang from racks
& whistle
mice children in a dream

no recreation this duende
but a blue fist shaking this duende

the man goes from the woman
in the plane, the seats
fill with mice

no candelabrum this duende
but a short fuse this duende

in the candle's eye
a mouse shines
under a mouse moon

no vulnerability this duende
but everything vulnerable this duende

where the mice die
the egg falls
in a garden of lost mice

no good mornings this duende
but the dream repeated this duende

the cat surrenders to
her mouse love
cries at the jailhouse door

no moon no teeth this duende
but no teeth no moon this duende

my blue love hides in cardboard
covers my belly
with her mice

no maestro sending messages this duende
but everyone receiving a message this duende

your finger is a mouse,
señora,
a mouse bathes in your violin

no ending known for this duende
but the coming end of this duende

duende fallen silent
this duende
in a storm of mice

IMAGINAL GEOGRAPHY 8

pretending to be ash
or butter, pretending
at deepest
intersection   corners

of the fat room
a man living his whole life
cylindrically
adrift

running with his animal
over the square
arena
the hut of shadows

near which the dancers turn
return & find
interior
delights

their dream time city
in a glass
a ball of light
sweet medicine, o

red & yellow
break against the ash
butter that hides
my fingers

hides me also
where it registers
the temperature
of floods & rooms

AIRPLANE SONGS

(first set)

1

I am so crazy for you
Captain Star
Your talk is like my radio
you listen
badly
Walk under the lightning
Captain
& strike it
rich & crazy
This song will bring you to the top

2

He struggles with a song
he can't dislodge
—or can he?—
"I was alive & stupid
"like your eyes
"Sweet angel
"rock my boat
"this is the long road to
"satisfaction

3

The top of the Hit Parade
once was exciting
like riding on an airplane's back
I wish it was that exciting again
(it won't be!)

4

The plane rocks
back & forth
& up & down
the city is a little city
—was it once big?—
& the people gone from you
Their dust is only
the edge of paradise
in back of the magellanic clouds

(second set)

1   A HASID FROM BELZ

with whom I speak
high in the DC–10
& waiting at door of
Men's Room
—you from Brooklyn?
—yeah
—how many Jews in San Diego?
I dunno
can't count them
lots of Jews

2

He pulls old words from me:
my grandfather
a hasid at the court in Radzymin
not Rizhyn
& he knows
the smile acknowledges the fact
—the fact is senseless—
o Belz of Kafka
Belz of Jiri Langer
golden nights

3

now the plane is over Iowa
it blurs
the oranges of California
like the stars of Belz

ALTAR PIECES

1

if the world should collapse
little king
it would go down with you
into the hole

you make darkness & I make darkness
it's all the same
somebody comes out of it
the suckers go back in

2

beautiful men &
beautiful women
come alive

we are at the beginning of
a dream
someone will have to write

the great book of the century
assembled
as dream-work

the authors move like children
into death
dancing like children

to feel this deeply, as an eye
over the silver counter

the table where a bishop sits
counting the near leaves

the sound of money vanishing
a "one" pasted in place

a "two" over the bishop's eye
to frame a painting

like a life   it is
a sappy proposition

in the rain   the figure seated
on the "three"

becomes a further space man
red & howling

a bishop like a garden
at the far edge of space

3 / Altar Pieces

WAR

. . . .

he is (they say) a general with tits
down to his knees
he whom they call "the mother"
whose knobs they pinch
stifflegged & lonely
like a cloud adrift
past maps of Italy
bunkers where he swallows
the macho fluids
hates the sexual residue
but thrives from it
in the collapse of centuries
the generals
still up to their tongues in shit
demand it
in their talk   frail jaws
& squeaking old man voices
carry across the room
the war   not real
the death of boys   a caution
he is the bride the others sell
at weddings   at parades
he inches past the other generals
hungry fingers spread apart
under their tongues
beckons the young men to his breasts
& prongs them
electric emissions from his radios
go forth   electric flags
& well-flanged lady admirals
shadow his nuts
the immaculate delivery begun
he sings the memory of his lost tubes
blue uterus

the birth of perfect soldiers
mother warriors
a hissing army slides
under his ponds   its bugles
sound a single "h"
deflowered   dreaming
the general drops from a winged motorcycle
over Asia
rides past a dozen skies
spent veins ejaculating
milk   blue sperm
over his eyelids
the corners of his mouth turned down
in gratitude
his blue teeth colored red
the shreds of boy flesh hang from
shining below his gums
the generals spangle each other's stars
they bow to him
at sundown   in the fishlight
"my flank (he croaks) is tubular
"my hand is at your spine
"the ants climb your medulla
"where the sand burns
"orange
"pink
"the final rodeo's in town
"even the clowns ride bareback
"truth comes slowly
"if it would come at all
the wagging old tongues squirm   the squads
resume encounters
in a hole a wormy mattress
where an old man like a goddess squats
the young boys fondle
his dry tits
he dreams old wars & new ones
hears the sly plunk of mandolines
over the Gulf of Suez

HUNGER

1

the prisoners, committed to death
around the world
the squadrons of hungry ghosts almost like armies
that swarm up & down the streets
always behind your house
never in front
where the bright wall tells the world
"a happy giant lives here"
I would rather run away
no more terror & no more loss of memory
promises the guard
I tell him: I don't want any part of this
even if it's a dream—& it is—
in the blood the enzymes are the same
the prisoners are all marching & won't stop
until they lay you flat
until your eye—no longer focused on the road
no longer on the sign over the supermarket
illumination—flops on your cheek
the jaw at a cockeyed angle
away from your face, the skin
peculiar, pasty like a kind of earth
loose & crumbling
what will you become & what will we all become
before the time of the big change
the miracle?
the body is a remorseless institution
it escapes me though I respect it
greatly, though I equate it with this poem
another metaphor for death
the armies of the world have no respect
for flesh
        they run their wheels
over it, they crush it to shadows
with their wheels

the hunger of the rich man
knows no end
the man & the woman, both insatiable
reduce the world's flesh to a sauce
& smear it over their wrists & thighs
& follow the delicious cracks of their bodies
trying to shove the substance in
a gibelotte done hunter style
the dead feet still thick with fur
the tongues torn from their cries
harbor the ghosts of tears
wild capers scrape the bourgeois flesh
the hunger of the man & woman
lords of hunger
gives a direction to their lives
they speak in French
the only language the bones understand
when they rub the femurs against each other's nipples
—hungry hungry—
when his own mouth over her cunt
feels the dead bone slip in
from his trembling fingers
this is how gods make love in graveyards
eating, sucking out their lives
the woman mother of the bones straddles
a throne of hungry beggars
hands reach up to her in death
they stroke her ribs
incite her, the man & woman
gather strength
under the shadow of an egg-beater
a new vibrator, watching
"les viandes roties, the eloquence
"of slowly turning flesh
"contracting
"swelling
"fondled by repeated basting

"assumes a rich brown satin glaze
the hunger of the rich man
leaves him shrunken
because it doesn't end
he says "sweet momma," croons it
in the voice that made him famous
they eat each other's sex
then they eat the sex of others
they invent new hungers
hunger for power & for grass
hunger for sleep & badges
hunger for swollen sausages
hunger for swollen legs
hunger for the sounds of swollen children
hunger for omens
hunger for facades
hunger for kings
hunger for irreversible death
hunger for a monument to hunger
only the rich can still invent
they wait for future hungers
servants will spoon for them
they drive to funerals & spas
they leave crisp dollars on each other's plates
the hunger of the rich man
reaches for the moon
it breaks the world in half
& hands it
first to his bride, his love
they melt in tears
the band plays "satisfaction"
but they go on eating
"till the end of time"

TERROR

. . . .

dream of the jews
has ended   something else
waits in its place
a gunman maybe
standing at your door
who watches
in back of his blood
the horse's eye
run through his mind
"a wolf" the killer
calls himself
offers his body, shyly
to the fathers
wakes at dawn, his eye
bigger than the moon
shines for him
& leads him down the hall
—hellos, exchange of dishes
fantasies of home—
the mouth of the fanatic
trembles   stutters
he is in love with his first dream
the taste of honey
cloth against fingertips
the traditions of their people
motors secret hideouts
his mother even now
whispers to his dark side
the letters of the universe
exploding lights
signal him on
he will address the bride
again   a lesson of his courage
he will give her

satisfaction
night & day
he circles around her
like a watchdog
prowling prowling
beside her father's stall
the gunman
speaks to his own shadow
on the hill
—depletion—
—death—
over the hill a camel
walks, stupidly
into the camera
stop him!
even if for a moment
cries the gunman's mouth
the teeth of the fanatic
biting staining the pale roots
the mask of antiochus
finds a jewish face
looks back at us
in righteousness
in anger at his own flesh
what can we give
but whispers
to make the rain appear?
the rain won't,
will it?
the daughter returns to the hut,
party ended,
bodies propped on bare beds
the fanatic's kin
his victims
tunnels exploded through their hearts
fly past him
foam pours from his mouth
his lungs fill up with foam

the wounded deer flies past
& calls him
like his vanished thumbs
another landscape
opens
with his boot he presses
legs & back
moving the flesh aside
& probes—aloof—the thin line
where the legs meet
grown thick with hair
how tight the dreamer's hand
becomes   how close
to prayer
his angry copulations
the mind of the fanatic
fills with glass   the fish
swim in the broken auto
furniture & rags
ignited
clot the hallways
processions of pale jews
are arabs now
the gunman, dark fanatic
gentile become jew
jew gentile
bellows in broken hebrew
in accents of his childhood
southern towns
assassins & vigilantes
even his mother can't believe
the coming struggle
treasons against god
repelled
forever   the killer
born to kill
escapes from the viet nam tunnel
in the street of little jewelers

semites of his mind
he rides a hairy motor bike
(the friend says)
gun slung over chest
into a world of strangers
caftaned killers
heavy with arab names
who wait for him
will stage the final shootout
the clock is moving
toward its end
explosions at the father's grave
the decade is a thrill for them
a new encounter
bigger than the last
the blood is such a clock
& such a clock
is always throbbing
in the blood
& in the morning sky

On May 2, 1980, Palestinian gunmen ambushed a group of Israeli settlers on the occupied West Bank. Among the six Israelis killed was Eli Hazeez (the last name means "the wolf"), born James Eli Mahon, Jr., in Alexandria, Virginia. An American Protestant by birth, he came out of Viet Nam & American ultraconservatism into Israeli citizenship & conversion through the right-wing Kach movement led by Meir Kahane. During his stay in Israel, the *N.Y. Times* reported, "he was jailed for 8 months for breaking into Arab houses in Hebron, smashing furniture, beating residents, and shouting at them to get out of 'Jewish houses.'" Of those who died in the ambush, "he alone was buried defiantly in the Jewish Cemetery of occupied Arab Hebron."

STRIKE!

for j.h.

. . . . . .

against the workers' state
the true strike comes
& brings
            defeat
                        a giant snail
buried between the factory & the town
the melancholy slavic shadow of the true strike
in its eyes (o futuristy)
raises a battered rubber hood
over the gasworks
the little air that seeps under its sides
expands
& covers the workers' homes beneath
with fogs & dialectics
another victory over the sun
they add to   a last hope
that something may outlive this century
the mother in the film by Eisenstein
her babe
                  torn from her side
                                    on wheels
on tiny motors
that slip across the edge
—comrade descendants—
that leave the frame & roll
down the Odessa steps

a needle on the dial of a machine
a broken mirror
scatters the true strike, reflects
the calloused workers' hands hard-fisted
torches at palace entrance
fires in the gardens
where sentries warm their hands
fur caps & iron helmets
ammonia in their nostrils
Warsaw Petrograd Odessa
fused   the waves of workers
form a ninth wave
chain themselves to factory gates
again   suspenders
hanging from
                    crystal chandeliers
torn pages of a book that float
"like feathers in a Jewish pogrom"
o futuristy
the true strike lives in frozen squares
flashes of bright lights that form
pictures of the new world
wounded tongues
a language none have yet learned to speak
the dream of Kruchonykh
gone the prophecy of Khlebnikov
in ruins Mayakovsky
strangling between the giant legs
of Stalin   earthbound
like Tatlin's iron bird
the comrade bosses
                    mill around
                         in Poland
grey uniforms & blaring eagles
of the workers' state
the sadness of the slavic past
rekindled
still in their pale green eyes that watch

the true strike rise again
kabbala in the shipyards
Jack
    in Petrograd a sailor lobs
his first bomb down the chimney
in Warsaw it explodes
six decades later
like a prophecy
        a ball of fire
            sparks
blown senselessly around the world
each one a spirit-
general the seeds of generals
to come   a million generals
enthroned   clusters of generals
sent spinning
hovering over the workers' houses
descending into mines
& shipyards
the hungry everywhere
the police & generals
in every corner of the earth
Christ in chains
in fury
the workers' revolution
has become   the true strike
turned against the true strike
you remember & call back to me
in mystic slavic letters
a cyrillic outcry
the comrade madmen pissing in the street
at the foot of some black ikon

EUROPE

for Pierre Joris

mind   the gap
the sign at Clapham Junction
reads, the train
pulls out for death
the messenger called Satan
in the sour pub
time-honored
pilgrim
with toes jamming the bar-rail
hoists his pint
a yard over his skull
the suds stream
moistly
the street dissolving
into Europe   mystics
& dead rabbis
circuits of generations follow
the Belgian factories like ghosts
behind us   do we ride
the train, asleep
the passengers tangled in our dreams
where spiders become birds
birds lunge at us
angry but thoughtful   never
bite us   on the Rhine
sadly inflating with the generations
we move beyond
old Dutchmen
searching for nails in shallow water
"it is impractical"
the mother says   she cannot
lace their shoes
forever   while the children cry
the Dadaists in exile

somewhere in these fields
o LONDON ONION
bring us the death of Europe
the news delivered
fair & square
echoes the Europe in their eyes
the tongue protruding
Europe that cries for nooky
like a king   a shadow monarch
his lusts played out against the helpless
maidens & slaves
the energies of empire
dipping
only his memories remain
he gobbles up old photographs
the dukes of Luxembourg
gremlins of Zanzibar beneath his bed
an eyelash trembling
clogging their rosy stews
sad Europe   lover
presses a finger down her throat
they kiss & vomit
often   men with bowties
women wrapped up in colored beads
& gauzes
lost in the other century
the journey through the stones
of Stonehenge   cathedral
towns & tea rooms
now manned by strangers
Dada ghosts
with dreadlocks   Europe's tongue
stuck to his gums
his failure to conceive a language
haunts him   it is five o'clock
again the lights go out
a Turkish heaven
rises near the bahnhof

the future is no closer
than it ever was
the mind is searching for the mind
hello, tomorrow
sing our lips
the foxy face of Europe
—now my own face—
smiles down on us   across the gap
old trickster for another day
another avatar
gone down the drain

Bastille Day
1981

YAQUI 1982

"the eye of performance is cruel"
—H. Blau

1

the jews of ceremony
dance in the thin sand of
pascua pueblo   in their pinhole
eyes new fires start
watched by ourselves & others
the bright memory of days to come
tomorrow   but the face
back of the mask
is fathomless
the jews march through the night
clack-clack their sticks
speak for them
red & white
the tips like dagger points
& voiceless
they are the purveyors of the death of jesus
yaqui-style
they stomp & whip each other
thursdays   the master jew
baldheaded man with droopy eyes
& half-a-beard
fresh crown of thorns over his ears
squats by the cross
black-coated
in white jodhpurs
it is the man without the belt
(el viejito)
who seeks the heart of jesus
in a box
white-covered
with lines of green above

74

the flat red heart
& silver rays
he looks into & sees
a crucifix   a water bottle
flowers & candles
then bangs his sticks
together   in a trance
they lead him with a silky rope
pinned to his shoulders
jews & clowns
how beautifully they walk
the stations of the cross
in yaqui
the plaza stretches to infinity
where the smallest freak is jesus
& the angels sing

2

                                        "you smile & the angels sing"
                                                —traditional

judas coyote rages
at altar   cracks
twin sticks for language
when the bell rings—
the virgin dangling
overhead—her name
her residue of fat he wipes
mindless down his thigh
mad dog mad judas
the first to poke his snout
under the altar
to sniff the linens on
the dead man's crotch
behind him packs of jews erupt

stalking the dead man's tracks
like flies
mad pharisees & litvocks
goat-faced dada jews
banging a klezmer tomtom
fiddles & accordions
they strum & dance to
faggot jews who hump each other
military jews
& jewish sheriffs
a pulpy cherub jew who bellows
an apache jew a lizard a highstepping jew
a nigger jew who chews a stogie
an arab jew with hiccups
a jew who dies of constipation
a two-headed jew
a jew without a nose
a jew who rolls by in a perfect sphere
a troop of jews with bells on
brushing past us, touching
the coyote jew who walks beside
a second jew like jesus
like judas riding backwards
on a mule
feet dangling
forehead aglow & bald
the body of the martyr
red with ants
astride the universe
they face & shake their hips
the accountant & the dog of heaven
whom we watch here
in the full moon over tucson
a true vision of the cross
they give us
comic deaths felt down the ages
judas burning
maestro who keeps the catholic

maestro's dribble
from our ears

3

only the clown plays jesus
here   the other jesus
remaining in wood or plaster
he is laid out in purple gowns
his bier is like
a birthday cake from which
a doll emerges
the babe's head of the other poems
to grace our dreams   it is
the ordinary insanity of art
my dear anselmo
enchanted worlds
we have all touched
on the green side of your purple house
in tucson   a white leaf
is very real
it has grown by leaps over the winter
(someone writes)
& fills the deep well
next to the cloud pump
stalking so slowly the deer
dancer advances
that the church bursts with
anticipation
(someone else writes)
"trust the world to little max"
& if I do
seamlessly across the canyon rides
the dada financier
his head a squash
his heart a breadbox
with a mechanic's gift for flowers
he will match you

world for world anselmo
wheels & axles
thrown into the air to make them
sing   a dentist's drill
a meat grinder
the mist on railroad tracks
will fly around him
headlights will be deformed
—zimbrabim—
will light up shoes
& nylon hair
we will prepare our voyage to the desert
the flower world
anselmo
where a crazed stewardess will bring us
both a tray
a dish shaped like a funnel
a delay in glass that holds
a single eyeball

THE LITTLE SAINT OF HUAUTLA

for Maria Sabina

lives to be too old:
her voice
painful to her chest
echoes
until her belly sags
cries to the tumor
under her heart:
"o you moon child
"you little eye of god
"little birds that grow
"from trees
the drunk beside us
—young man
sans teeth—
who stumbles
to reach her hilltop
sits by the saint
& hiccups
"are you a saint?" he asks
"I am a governor" she tells him
"I am a clock
"a wheel
"the palsy in the judge's fingers
"flutters my skirts
"I am the moon
"I welcome my dizziness
"I chew the little things
"& whistle
"you will eat your eyes
"—the clock says—
"your shadows
"will slide down your throats
"will choke you

"you will come back to my hillside
"flying   martyrs
"will bang tibetan bells
"the mountain god
"little king on horseback
"will cut you down
the saint says
hides behind her lost teeth
the face of Krishna
smiles back at us
her own face in a glow
of cigarette smoke
as we make
small talk
small mirrors shine from
the robes of all saints
Mexico in summer
still wet with fruit
the garbage of poor lives
poor women know
their huipils bright with birds
& butterflies
flowers of the orange dance
—o mystic weddings—
where in Huautla de Jimenez
we were the last to come
the bus still bringing
freaks from Mexico
to eat the sour mushrooms
with earth & goat shit
wild on their lips:
this is language
tiny letters
so brilliant in the sky
of *la sierra mazateca*
where we arrive
to meet our tiger shamans
looking for their tracks

their footprints
like whirlwinds in far cities
torn from the earth
o clocks
o eagles
for you the sweat of Christ
Christ's semen
becomes a plant
transparent flower
glowing in ocean
someone walking with
Christ's flower
as a staff   a man
with money like a saint
general whose footprints leave
whole jewels
in our path
—she sings
searches for the night—
the drunk Indian
(poor boy)
smiles to her face
& hiccups
like a drum
his language dying in him
"are you a movie star?" he asks
"I am a calendar" she tells him
"I am a comet woman
"an oppossum
"I drink warm beer
"freshly I make my bed
"my photographs envelop Mexico
"I cackle like a turkey
"my voice is endless
"in museums where shawls are hanging
"in bars in fancy homes in ballrooms
"in concert with the grateful dead
"France awaits me

"the Italian directors come at night
"they suck my mushrooms
"the Pope come to Oaxaca with the others
"butlers are dancing with
"the brides of god
"brides of mountain men
"little kings on horseback
"Shiva's ikon dances
"on my altar
"clocks are dancing
"& oppossums
"wheels & governors
"in dreams without a word
"left to intone
she says   it says
for her
the book of language says
translated into broken Spanish
sold to feed the dead
the dying language
hiding from strangers' eyes
the way the mushrooms hide
withhold their language
will not speak
except when the children's voices
tell us:
casa
dinero
hongos
hidden from your eyes too
Maria poet of these hills
fast speaking woman
bought & sold
to feed the language of the rich
—cloaca of all languages—
—oppressors whom you love—
you hilltop woman
you saint woman

you clock woman
you moon woman
you martyr woman
you mirror woman
you tiger woman
you language woman
you flower woman
you money woman
you warm beer woman
you my mother shepherdess
(it says)
o mother of the sap (it says)
mother of the dew (it says)
mother of breasts (it says)
mother of the harvest
you rich mother
now standing visible & loud
before us
ha ha ha
so so so
so so so
hee hee hee
see see see
hum hum hum
it says & rises
lonely   lost
the spirit that wanders through America
saint children
disembodied in city air
crazy in Mexico
a squatters' village to hold the poor
fury of dead Mazatecs
the ghost of Juarez
speaking English
like my own voice
at your doorway
shaking this sad rattle
singing

without the hope of god
or clocks
with no word between us
veladas that cost
a thousand pesos
this vigil for your book
& mine
for any languages
still left to sell

Some New Directions Paperbooks

For complete listing request complete catalog from
New Directions, 80 Eighth Avenue, New York 10011   † Bilingual